MOUSE POOP OR BAT POOP?

By George Fittleworth

Gareth Stevens
PUBLISHING

Please visit our website, www.garethstevens.com. For a free color catalog of all our high-quality books, call toll free 1-800-542-2595 or fax 1-877-542-2596.

Cataloging-in-Publication Data

Names: Fittleworth, George.
Title: Mouse poop or bat poop? / George Fittleworth.
Description: New York : Gareth Stevens Publishing, 2020. | Series: The scoop on poop | Includes glossary and index.
Identifiers: ISBN 9781538233481 (pbk.) | ISBN 9781538229576 (library bound) | ISBN 9781538233498 (6pack)
Subjects: LCSH: Mice–Juvenile literature. | Bats–Juvenile literature. | Animal droppings–Juvenile literature.
Classification: LCC QL737.R6 F58 2019 | DDC 599.35'3–dc23

Published in 2020 by
Gareth Stevens Publishing
111 East 14th Street, Suite 349
New York, NY 10003

Designer: Sarah Liddell
Editor: Therese Shea

Photo credits: Cover, p. 1 Stephen Bonk/Shutterstock.com; p. 5 (main) Enrique Ramos/Shutterstock.com; p. 5 (inset) Photo - TMD/Shutterstock.com; p. 7 Landshark1/Shutterstock.com; p. 9 Michal Pesata/Shutterstock.com; p. 11 torook/Shutterstock.com; p. 13 Independent birds/Shutterstock.com; p. 15 Ivan Kuzmin/Shutterstock.com; p. 17 Ethan Daniels/Shutterstock.com; p. 19 (bat poop) Danupol Wongchai/Shutterstock.com; p. 19 (mouse poop) Rodgerjackman/Oxford Scientific/Getty Images.

Printed in the United States of America

CPSIA compliance information: Batch #CS19GS: For further information contact Gareth Stevens, New York, New York at 1-800-542-2595.

CONTENTS

Boldface words appear in the glossary.

A Mystery in the Attic

You're in the **attic** of your house. You see dark bits on the floor. Uh oh! Could it be mouse poop . . . or even bat poop? How can you find out? Let's learn more about these small animals.

More About Mice

Mice are small **mammals** in the animal group called **rodents**. There are more than 30 species, or kinds, of mice. The most common is the house mouse. Yes, house mice may live—and poop—in houses like yours!

House mice usually build their nests near food. They eat almost anything, including bugs, seeds, and people food. They eat 15 to 20 times a day! Mice are **nocturnal**. If you hear noises in the attic at night, it could be mice!

Mice are often thought of as pests. They get into people's homes, eat their food, and chew holes through things. You saw some chewed up old clothes in the attic. That might be a clue about what produced the poop!

A Bit About Bats

Like mice, bats are mammals. There are more than 900 species! They're usually gray, brown, or black. Small bats may measure just 6 inches (15 cm) from the tip of one wing to the other. Others measure 5 feet (1.5 m)!

13

Most bats are nocturnal. They fly around at night looking for bugs to eat. Some eat fruit and small animals. Vampire bats drink animals' blood! Bats use sounds and **echoes** that bounce back from objects to find their way around.

Bats rest during the day in dark places, such as caves, trees—and attics! They hang upside down while they roost, or sleep. Some bats live in groups of over 100! Luckily, you didn't see roosting bats in your attic.

Side by Side

It's time to compare their poop. Bat poop, called guano, looks like dark brown pieces of rice. It's often in a large pile. Mice poop looks like dark rice, too! It's usually spread out. There's also another difference. Bat poop smells bad!

BAT POOP

MOUSE POOP

19

Whose Poop?

Both bats and mice may be found in attics. Their waste looks **similar**. Which is in your attic? The poop was spread out, and it didn't smell. It was mouse poop! Now, it's time to get that mouse out of your house!

CONSIDER THE CLUES

	MOUSE	BAT
DOES IT LIVE IN ATTICS?	SOMETIMES	SOMETIMES
WHAT DOES ITS POOP LOOK LIKE?	DARK PIECES OF RICE	DARK PIECES OF RICE
IS THE POOP IN A PILE OR SPREAD OUT?	SPREAD OUT	PILE
DOES THE POOP SMELL?	NO	YES-BAD!

IT WAS THE MOUSE'S POOP! 21

GLOSSARY

attic: a room or space that is just below the roof of a building and that is often used to store things

echo: a sound that repeats because it bounces off an object

mammal: a warm-blooded animal that has a backbone and hair, breathes air, and feeds milk to its young

nocturnal: active at night

rodent: a small, furry animal with large front teeth, such as a mouse or rat

similar: almost the same as someone or something else

FOR MORE INFORMATION

BOOKS

Carr, Aaron. *Bats*. New York, NY: AV2 by Weigl, 2015.

Riggs, Kate. *Mice*. Mankato, MN: Creative Education and Creative Paperbacks, 2017

WEBSITES

Bat
animals.sandiegozoo.org/animals/bat
There's so much more to learn about bats here.

Bats
defenders.org/bats/basic-facts
Find out how bats use echoes to hunt.

Fun Mouse Facts for Kids
www.sciencekids.co.nz/sciencefacts/animals/mouse.html
Read more about the small mammals called mice.

INDEX